A Love Letter to Me:

Building Healthy Self-Esteem for Women and Girls

Petula Varsha

ISBN: 0615669492
ISBN-13: 978-0615669496

This book is dedicated to all the strong women who have come to recognize their own worth, in one form or another.

The hummingbird spirit animal symbolizes the enjoyment of life and lightness of being. Those who have the hummingbird as a totem are invited to enjoy the sweetness of life, lift up negativity wherever it creeps in and express love more fully in their daily endeavors. This fascinating bird is capable of the most amazing feats despite its small size, such as traveling great distances or being able to fly backwards. By affinity with the hummingbird, those who have this bird as totem may be encouraged to develop their adaptability and resiliency while keeping a playful and optimistic outlook

CONTENTS

ACKNOWLEDGMENTS

Many thanks to all the women who participated in the project. I appreciate their time and their candidness when sharing their stories with me. I would also like to give special thanks to my sister, Candice, who gave me great support throughout the creation of this book. She paved the way for me through the years, and provided mentorship and unconditional love when I needed it. A big thanks of gratitude to my dear friend Pon Angara for his continued support and amazing creativity in seeing my vision for the design of such a beautiful cover. Special thank you to a beautiful soul Steve Starr who is no longer with us, for making me look good in his unique talent to capture everyone's beauty through photography. Thank you to my wonderful marketing and PR assistant Burns Foster for keeping me on track. And, finally, a big thank you to Ridgely Dunn, who assisted in the editing and publication of this book. I couldn't have done this without her.

SANKARSINGH

FORWARD

"A Love Letter to Me" started as a pilot workshop for adolescent girls in inner city communities. The end result was so well received that the demand for the program grew almost overnight. In order to generate funding for the project, two fundraising campaigns were launched to create awareness and gain financial support to begin implementing this program throughout local communities, with the hope of eventually going nationwide. The basis of the program focuses on building healthy self-esteem for adolescent girls. The goal is to set achievable personal, social, and academic goals. We provide support by mentoring and using testimonies of and by women and girls who overcame adversity in their own lives. Part of this campaign included organizing and hosting wine and food pairing events which provided a venue for potential donors (individual and corporate) to attend and learn more about the program. The program has since continued to gain momentum, ultimately leading to the creation of this book, and the development of online seminars and instructional materials.

INTRODUCTION

"They had to prove that women were human. They had to shatter, violently if necessary, the decorative Dresden figurine that represented the ideal woman of the last century. They had to prove that woman was not a passive, empty mirror, not a frilly, useless decoration, not a mindless animal, not a thing to be disposed of by others, incapable of a voice in her own existence, before they could even begin to fight for the rights women needed to become the equals of men."
—Betty Friedan

As a woman, I know that the mere fact of my gender has presented obstacles, although I may have been unaware of them early in life. As I absorb the information and images inflicted upon me by modern media, I can see clearly that the oppression of women continues, despite any apparent advances to the contrary. It appears in many forms—from gender inequity on Wall Street and in the home, to outright slave labor conditions for women in other parts of the world. However, I take comfort learning about women of past generations who transcended society's rigid stereotypes in order to become heroes to us all.

It's scarcely imaginable that something as basic as a woman's right to vote wasn't ratified as an amendment to the U.S. Constitution until 1920. But in 1756, a little-known woman named Lydia Chapin Taft became the first recorded legal woman voter in America. Other women more prominent in popular history, including Amelia Earhart, Rosa Parks, Susan B. Anthony, Harriet Beecher Stowe, Billy Jean King, and Harriet Tubman, exercised their own powerful beliefs, needs, and aspirations within a set of social norms that told them they should be more concerned with home and hearth. These women overcame significant challenges in order to know and love themselves, and to become what they wanted to be. Because these women acted on the strength of their convictions, they blazed a trail for others who followed them. And although women's causes are more advanced now than they've ever been, generations of social inequality have left their mark: low self-esteem still mars the emotional and cognitive framework of many women.

As a result of various life challenges, poor self-concept can be a confusing, if somewhat veiled, aspect of our personalities. Raw emotions, unquestioned beliefs, and old wounds we are only partially aware of, can contribute to our decision making processes, for better or worse. We sometimes feel as if we aren't choosing our actions consciously, but are passive recipients of things happening to us. However, decisions which lead us down paths we do not find fulfilling do not necessarily have to seal our fates for the rest of our lives. Instead, obstacles can lead us to look deeply at the way we live, and in the process of looking, we may recognize that our primary opposition lies within.

In an effort to better understand my own challenges related to self-concept and self-esteem, I wanted to hear about situations faced by other women. As a result, I asked forty women to write about the hurdles they experienced from adolescence to middle age. As a result, they wrote about every kind of loss and pain, from racism and ethnocentrism, to bullying and domestic abuse. They shared how they mined knowledge and strength from the depths of their difficulties. These "love letters" are written to you, to your children, and to the writers' past, current, and future selves. Through their stories, we find inspiration to persevere in spite of setbacks, and discover that we are not alone in our experiences.

That said, I encourage you to open your heart as you read, so that you can connect with the words, and allow these stories to motivate and uplift you. These women shared their experiences so that through their hardships, you might come to believe in yourself and in what you are capable of achieving when you put your mind and your heart into your dreams. These letters take you from the youthful pangs of adolescent insecurities, through the journeys and missteps of early adulthood, and into middle age, where accumulated life experiences bring reflection and strength.

Through these letters, you can learn vicariously. In essence, the writers are sitting down with you and saying, "What you are going through now can be used as a tool to make you stronger, to prepare you for your life in the future." So whether you identify with the lost child, the single mother, or the business professional, every story lends proof that we all have the ability to develop our innate talents and define our own self-worth.

"What woman needs, is not as a woman to act or rule, but as a nature to grow, as an intellect to discern, as a soul to live freely, and unimpeded to unfold such powers as were given her..."
—Margaret Fuller

PART I
THE EARLY YEARS

1. Adolescence

"Adolescence is when girls experience social pressure to put aside their authentic selves and to display only a small portion of their gifts."
—Mary Pipher

When looking at the life stories collected here, it appears that many women's self-esteem issues stem from circumstances that developed in their early teen years. Never fully resolved, these issues may follow us into adulthood. As girls, many of the writers suffered poorly developed self-concepts, which made them more susceptible to the unrelenting social pressure of their peers. As teenagers with low self-esteem, they tended to focus on the negative aspects of themselves, as opposed to the more positive qualities of their personalities. Often, the women described feeling unworthy of being loved and accepted by others.

Balancing a desire to be accepted by peers, and yet at the same time remaining comfortable and true to oneself, is one of the most difficult challenges of adolescence and young womanhood. In attempting to live up to the standards they feel society, parents, boyfriends, and others have imposed on them, girls can step out of their comfort zones in a negative way. Unfortunately, some of the actions prompted by what is basically a desire to raise the self-esteem, can produce negative consequences that last a lifetime. By becoming familiar with these struggles in all their various disguises, we can help other women avoid the pitfalls we've encountered, and help ourselves continue to grow out of the rigid patterns that would otherwise stifle us through adulthood.

"High school was lonely. I wanted to feel like I belonged, so I did what my peers were doing. As I look back, I know following my peers led to bad decisions that greatly impacted my life."—Angela, age 29

"Wow, our first love. Remember him? The thought, idea and desperation that someone could love fat, ugly, bad skin, bad hair us...this desperation would eventually chase this love and many others away; it would lead us to experience physical and mental abuse from "our love," all because we wanted someone to love us, all because we could not believe someone could love us, all because we had no love for ourselves. Remember?"—Rebecca, age 36

For teenage girls with low self-esteem, the line between right and wrong can appear blurry. They find themselves doing things that they otherwise would not, just to gain the approval of the group.

"It wasn't cool to do well in school; I was always a straight A student in grammar and junior high school. However, if I wanted to fit in, I had to 'dumb it down.' I started cutting classes and not studying to hang out with friends."
—Stephanie, age 37

Low self-esteem can overshadow a girl's better judgment; in these cases, because their appraisals of self-worth are so reliant on what the group thinks of them. Teen girls may find themselves in situations where they give into undesired sexual advances because a weak sense of self does not allow them to say no.

"I was 16, and definitely not ready for the complicated emotions that sex brings, but all of my friends were doing it. I hated it, but couldn't say no. I wanted him to stay with me. After a while, I thought I loved him, [but] was I really capable of understanding love? I should have spent more time engaging in age-appropriate activities, exploring and discovering my identity."—Elizabeth, age 42

Transitioning from elementary to middle school is one of the scariest and most significant times in a young person's life. This step takes each of us on our own unique journey as we learn how to fit in. It is a swift evolution we have to make; experiencing so much within such a short period of time, it is hard to fathom how anyone emerges without scars. During this phase, it is the exceptional, the most attractive or athletic kids, who soar to the top. Their previous achievements bolster their personal outlooks while others sneak away, trying to go unnoticed. Others, like Theresa, seek to find their identities. Those with positive demeanors, or in Theresa's case, a humble comedian's self-deprecating style, can use these traits as an avenue to acceptance; even if it wasn't the most fantasized of social labels, it was a means of finding a place to fit in.

"The thought of entering the high school years left us full of fear and even more insecure. You must remember how we thought the best way to hide our pain would be to crack the joke on our self before others had the opportunity, or to act like a bully, somehow hoping to instill fear in others, but we forgot we were labeled "Scaredy Cat" in our grade and middle school years, and no matter how hard we tried, that name would stick worse than the best Elmer's glue. But being funny, now being funny worked! So we attract and make friends quickly, even obtaining the nickname "Crazy Tee," along with many others: "Thunder Thighs," "big lips," and the all-time classic, "Fofo," said with giggles and laugh as the culprit tried to reach out for a tap on our fore head. Every day we laughed out loud, every night we cried within. Remember?

The desire to perform, act, and be dramatic was something we've always been great at, but the insecurity of shining too bright kept that light dim. The poetry reading and drama awards left us feeling so beautiful within, only temporary, but beautiful nonetheless." —Theresa, age 28

Joann is another voice of encouragement. Although she also struggled with her self-concept, it was by learning to be herself that she gained tremendous success:

"Be who you are and others will help you. I know it feels like being who you are got you into this mess, but it didn't. I know that you feel completely unworthy. I know you feel like you must make others happy for them to love you. I know if I say anything to the contrary, you won't believe me. But know that others will and do love you. You are so smart. You are going to be the president of an organization. You are going to run departments and own your own successful business. People are going to seek you out and ask for your opinion and help.

You are going to have two strong, smart daughters, and a marriage that feeds you and nurtures you. You and your sister are going to become close friends. And the abuse will stop. It will stop partly because you finally told someone, and that someone is a man who now loves you more than you ever thought you deserved to be loved. But you do." —Joann, 35 years old

2 Desire to Please

"Oh, God, I struggle with low self-esteem all the time! I think everyone does. I have so much wrong with me, it's unbelievable!"
—Angelina Jolie

During childhood, self-esteem is influenced particularly by acceptance from parents. Children with healthy self-esteem feel that their parents care about them and accept them for who they are. Parents who communicate these feelings consistently, through both word and action, help foster high self-esteem in their children. Alternatively, parents who communicate in a negative style can generate poor self-concepts in their children. Belittling remarks and threats are examples of negative communication that if used routinely are believed to lower self-esteem and diminish a child's feelings of love and acceptance. The child who does not feel her parents' love unconditionally, and apart from her accomplishments or achievements, can develop a personality style constructed to gain peer and parental approval.

Emily, a 37-year-old architect, looks back on her

childhood and shares how striving for perfection, and the need to fill the void of parental approval, led her to make bad decisions, setting up a series of complex events that kept her in a cycle of emotional instability. It wasn't until her late twenties that she discovered the root of her problem:

"Nothing I did was ever good enough for my mother. She never congratulated me for my successes and was hard on me for my failures. I was not good enough for my mother to love me. I had to be perfect to win the love of my mother. As I grew older, I felt like I had to be perfect to win the love of anyone. The pursuit of perfection consumed me. I was lost. I felt empty."—Emily, age 37

After years of wading through seas of depression, many women find themselves adrift in despair as they allow their past experiences to motivate them to solitude. However, there are some resilient types like Debra, who step away from previous esteem issues, and evolve to find strength and wisdom at their core. Debra writes:

"Today I am 56 years old, and I'm sitting here in my size 12 red leather dress, composing this letter. For me, the issue of self-esteem revolved around my weight my whole life. To this day, my 78 year old dad has no idea the impact his words had on me as a young child, and at this point he doesn't need to know. My self-esteem is no longer tightly wrapped around the outer appearance. I now enjoy life, love the way I look, and I know how to be happy even with a few extra pounds on! I have had a successful tailoring business for 28 years, and am proud of the work I have done in my personal life. I now have the ability to help others look their best. And now I just hear: 'Debra is so pretty,' with a period at the end."— Debra, age 56

Many letters in this book reflect complicated relationships and difficulties at home. With Marianne however, we see a single father with a supportive family structure, raising a daughter on his own. The father-daughter relationship is a powerful dynamic, and the development of personal strength is often reflective of this relationship. Marianne adjusted well and, despite her grades, maintained a sense of personal self-worth and a desire to achieve something better.

"As you enter high school you will meet more people who have lost more than you, and [yet] move forward and are achieving, and you begin to desire to be a better person, and stop using excuses to prevent you from achieving what you are intended to do, and from that you learn there is a light at the end of every tunnel, a lesson that you will go back to and pull from for the rest of your life.

In high school, you go on to be a member of Law and Society, Speech and Debate, run track, [become a] student government officer, and in your last year, captain of the cheer squad. Now that you have stopped using your circumstances as an excuse not to accomplish anything in life, you will begin to flourish as a young woman, a student (well, kind of), and a community activist. You learned the expression "to whom much is given, much is required," and work to make your community a much better place.

Though a touch of that lazy student is in you, and you battle within your intellectual ability and bare-minimum-to-get-by attitude, and it is a 4 year fight. Let me not lie, you will fight with yourself on this the rest of your life. The inner battle winds up with your scoring a 29 on your ACT, but having a 2.0 GPA, allowing you to get into some historically Black Colleges, but preventing you receiving any scholarship money. The test scores and your sorry GPA just don't match. Test scores may not measure intelligence if you don't score well, but if you score well most seem to concur it reflects an ability to get more than all C's.

High School ends up being the best years of your life. Your Grandmother remains in North Carolina, but constantly flies to see you and you back to see her. Your Aunts and Uncles help your single dad, and you truly have an entire village as a part of your cheering section. It's time to go to college."—Marianne, age 31

3 Desire to Fit in With Peers

"An individual's self-concept is the core of his personality. It affects every aspect of human behavior: the ability to learn, the capacity to grow and change. A strong, positive self-image is the best possible preparation for success in life."—Dr. Joyce Brothers.

"Tears gently fall from my eyes as I recall all the pain filled days in grade school and junior high, when eczema and coke bottle glasses took over the external self, leaving the internal self feeling ugly and unloved. The taunting and teasing from boys and girls only added to the pain within. I can remember holding back tears so the teasing would stop, not realizing it was only increasing the insecurity that would grow along with us in the years to follow."
—Illiana, age 34

Illiana is not the only person to have suffered these sorts of problems; likely surrounding her were others with similar difficulties. As a young adult, it is difficult to see behaviors outside our own personal boundaries. These boundaries slowly close around us until the only focus we have is ourselves. We cannot recognize the pain others are in, nor can we see a way out of our own pain by seeking the support of our peers. Illiana's despair is no different from that of millions of teenagers today, even though a generation has passed.

Negative feedback from peers has a similar effect as opinions from a parent. The child begins to believe the negative evaluations as truth about her self-worth. She starts to feel down, generally unsuccessful, and overwhelmed by the tasks of life. She tends to be shy, to remain where she feels safe, and to look for ways of escaping unpleasant realities or situations. Her low self-esteem contributes to the development of a false self, and a profound feeling of emptiness. Heather, just four years younger than Illiana, encountered the same obstacles, but viewed them as challenges. Although she wishes they hadn't happened, she recognizes their importance. She realizes how they affected her later in life, and how they empowered her to be a stronger person.

"I wish I could shield you from disappointments you experience, provide you with the right choices each time you are faced with difficult decisions, protect you from any form of hurt, harm, or danger, as you transition from girl to woman. But the truth of the matter is that I cannot. I cannot prevent you from experiencing all of the challenges that you will confront in life. And although life doesn't come with a compass, it is not impossible to navigate. Despite what may have happened in your past, I want you to know that you are beautiful and capable of doing whatever you set your mind to, what you're willing to work for. It doesn't matter where you were born or where you live, the success of your future is not limited to where you came from.

So dream…dream big. Learn what it takes to make your dreams a reality, and pursue them relentlessly. In life, things don't always go as planned, but don't be discouraged and don't give up. It's guaranteed that you will make mistakes, but as long as you learn from those mistakes, the experience will only make you stronger. Be encouraged, never settle for less than you deserve, and trust yourself."—Heather, age 30

Illiana and Heather had similar experiences growing up, and as we see below, another woman obviously troubled by bullying also found her way by learning from past experiences and building her own self-confidence. Although maintaining confidence is difficult among constant tribulations, her model of focusing on the positives is a good example of how to guide yourself on a meaningful and confident path:

"It was difficult to get up every morning, knowing what the day held for me—teasing, bullying, and the persistent emotional turmoil of wanting to fit in. How do I find the courage to just be me, when I know it will lead to loneliness, [and] feeling like an outcast? My advice to you is to explore different things, and engage in activities that you are interested in, and focus your energy on that."
—Kirskis, age 34

Life experiences affect change on many levels: the body changes in response to increasing levels of sex hormones; the thinking process changes as the teenager is able to think in a more abstract way; the social life changes as new people and peers come into range. These obstacles are made all the more difficult with teasing, as seen in Illiana's reference to "coke-bottle glasses," and other variables— obesity, acne, and other physical characteristics—that others capitalize on in an effort to encourage their own popularity.

While most of the letter writers were affected by self-esteem issues, many overcame these challenges as they stepped into new roles as adults. Whether they entered this new life phase with the help of peer encouragement, a new support system, or by turning their desires into reality, they were able to achieve what, at fourteen years old, seemed impossible. As adults, we sometimes forget that we also faced challenges, and that we were able to overcome many of them.

Over the years, there have been many self-help books designed to encourage positive thinking. The one which arguably affects the most people is the series *Don't Sweat the Small Stuff*. It's a small book, often hidden within the drawers of dressers and work desks as a calm reminder of what really matters, and often times what really doesn't matter. The book's author, Richard Carlson, suggests it may be helpful to ask yourself, "Will this matter one year from now?" It's a difficult task to ask someone who isn't used to questioning what's going on around them, but it's a good question to reflect upon. What were you doing last year at this time? Or try to think of a difficult situation. Does that situation still affect you today? The vast majority of our problems in life are temporary frustrations, yet we allow those frustrations to persist until they begin to color our daily lives.

As we have seen in this chapter, obstacles are commonplace in adolescence. However, by learning to focus on our own self-worth and the potential each situation offers for personal betterment and self-empowerment, we can turn obstacles into surmountable challenges which buoy us through more troubling and stressful circumstances.

4 Physical Image

"The best and most beautiful things in life cannot be seen, not touched, but are felt in the heart."—Helen Keller

Children today are inundated with media images that present an idealized standard of beauty and elegance. Media representations of beauty epitomize an image that few women will ever attain. Seeing these images over and over frequently leads girls to think that their own bodies are not acceptable, ultimately resulting in the development of an unhealthy body image. Unfortunately, such negative feelings can consume already fragile self-esteem. In reflection, we find where our true beauty lies, and what its source is. One writer, Serena, expresses these thoughts:

"I always felt that you had to be tall, thin, blonde, and have blue eyes to be beautiful. I certainly was not that. I never felt pretty, I was too fat, and had bad skin, and black hair. I felt ugly and constantly looked for acceptance. Looking back, I realized that I was wrong. I was actually pretty because I was different. It wasn't until I got older that I realized this. I found people who appreciated my unique beauty."—Serena, age 27

Below, Colette describes a medical condition that affected her physical appearance. The hurt she experienced in childhood remains with her to this day. However, she was able to channel that emotion into her career, enabling her to identify with and work with disabled children.

"Do you remember the great hair loss? I do, as a little girl used to having her pigtails pulled by the boys in church, and looking forward to the weekend, when it was time to have my hair braided for the upcoming school week. I remember crying when it began to fall out in handfuls. I remember holding in tears as mom had to cut it all off to even things out, and apply medication to my scalp, which was covered with eczema. I know mom was hurting about the cut, so I wanted to appear strong.

I cried silently for years as the kids called me names. I covered my head up 24 hours a day, first with a scarf, then a JJ-style D-Y-N-O-M-I-T-E hat. Remember how we wished our life would just come to an end? In those moments, we thought we were put on earth to be teased and taunted, often asking God, "Why did [you] make me ugly, and take all my hair away, leaving us with 'elephant skin' (that's what the kids called it)? I cried daily within..."
—Colette, age 42

Miriam did not step away from the young woman she was; instead, she sought out what represented who she wanted to be. While others tried to grow up too quickly and involved themselves in dangerous situations, Miriam devised a plan to remain who she was from the start, and to value her strengths and her personality:

"During my childhood years I was faced with every stereotype of a misfit that an adolescent could be labeled with in school. I was overweight, had severe acne, very thick glasses, I was not the best dressed, and, to top it all off, my parents were strict to the tenth degree. It was so bad that I could not even cross the street in front of my house without asking for permission, so going to parties or any social activity was out of the question. I definitely did not feel pretty and I was not in the popular crowd.

Because of my 'challenges' I was a very quiet student, and kept to myself most of the time. I did not feel comfortable in social settings at all. In order to overcome my 'challenges,' I had to decide what type of life I wanted to live. I would read the Sweet Valley High books and dream about living the lives that those students had. I quickly determined that life is what you make it. Although on the outside I did not like my appearance, I knew that I was beautiful on the inside. Everyone loved my personality and spirit. I didn't want to be sad and have a boring life, so I surrounded myself with other students who could relate to me. We formed our own group and started coming up with our own fun activities. We would have makeover parties; create our own dance clubs in the basement, and various other activities.

I realized that I could change my outer appearance as well by doing things within my control. I had my parents purchase acne medicine, I found new ways to make my clothing look more fashionable, and I begged my parents for contact lenses. I was still overweight, but eventually I was able to lose weight and feel better about myself. I also had a group of friends who liked me for who I was, and accepted my perceived 'challenges.' I am now a social butterfly.

My advice to young girls growing up today is to love yourself for who you are at this very moment in time. There may be things that you don't like about yourself, or even your surroundings, but you do have control over your own happiness. If you feel like an outcast, surround yourself with positive people who have similar interests as you. Start your own social groups and activities. If you don't like the way you look, figure out a look that works for you and brings out your inner light.

Always remain true to who you are. Society does not define you; only you can define you! Everyone has his or her own uniqueness to add to the world, and you don't want to miss out on your life's purpose worrying about what others think. The joy is also in the journey. I truly believe that I experienced the things I did as a young adult so that I can be the person I am today. It has humbled me, and taught me to appreciate true friendships, as well as to honestly see my inner beauty."—Miriam, age 30

No matter what our age or stage of development, it is virtually impossible to control what we ingest in terms of media; our brains are flooded with it from the moment we step out of our homes, to when we return at night. Billboards and subway advertisements, magazines and television shows, even the products we buy; all conspire to convey images of who we should or could be if we were just a little better than our current selves. With so many voices speaking at once, it's often hard to listen to that inner voice, the one that is uniquely you, who cares only for your personal happiness and fulfillment. As a 16 year old girl, Joann remembers learning to identify her own voice in the midst of all the others, a voice which conveyed to her the wisdom of lessons learned, lessons which she now passes on to her daughters and other women:

"Embrace what YOU are good at. That is what I want my daughters to hear. That is what I want every girl today to hear. There are so many messages in magazines and music and television about girl you should be. You are told what size you should be, what books you should read, and what talents you should have. Listen to your own voice. What brings you joy? What do you do that makes time fly by? What is a skill that you want to nurture?

You are worthy. You are unique. Be with people who nurture you. Be with people who appreciate you for who you are. If your friends right now don't nurture and support you, find new ones that do. Don't settle just to fit it. Love yourself more than that. There are women all around this world who want to support you and love you and help you become the woman you were meant to be."
—Joann, age 35

Many of the letters submitted for this book focused on the struggles of growing up, and being teased or viewed as different if we were not tall, slim, and beautiful. By now, it should be clear that none of us are truly alone in our experiences, but is there a way to immunize ourselves and other women against the "epidemic" of low self-esteem? In the next segment, Sara describes how she was able to accomplish just that with a good support system, rather than languish over her lack of socially-accepted beauty:

"I had always been 'big–boned.' but thankfully my mom and grandmother were fashion plates, and taught me how to dress to cover flaws and accentuate the good. My grandmother was an excellent seamstress and made a lot of my clothes. She made me styles which were complementary to my size and shape, and I believe she bought smaller patterns (to make me feel good) and then cut them bigger so they would fit.

Watching her sew, I was mesmerized by how effortlessly she made the garments just by looking at the pictures. Somehow, when I was eight years old, I picked up a needle and thread, and began to make clothes for my Barbie dolls.

I think that the sewing talent runs in the family, because although my mom is not a seamstress, she knew the mechanics of sewing, and basically taught me the 'right way' to do it. Many times, she would watch me complete something, and then tell me to rip it out and start over. She told me I would learn to love sewing, or to hate it, but either way, I would learn to do it correctly.

In the years that followed, I graduated to making my own clothes and being 'plus-sized,' I tried to create clothes that were unique and one-of-a-kind, so as to take the attention off of my size, and it worked. People seemed to notice the clothes rather than my shape. Gradually my self-esteem improved as I continued to receive accolades for my uniqueness. Through the years, I worked for clothing stores and eventually got interested in designing clothes and hand-painting fabrics to sell."—Sara, age 26

Assignment#1: The letters in this first chapter reflect on the myriad conflicts and life experiences a girl can encounter in her early development. In the following space or in your own journal, choose one of the topics covered which speaks to your own situation as an adolescent. If you can, recall the questions your younger self wondered about at the age where you experienced the greatest difficulty. After you complete this short letter, write a second letter from your mature perspective that explores those questions, and answer them in your new voice.

A LOVE LETTER TO ME

PART II
RACIAL/ETHNIC/FAMILIAL
DIFFERENCES

1 Racial Issues

"I have a great belief in the fact that whenever there is chaos, it creates wonderful thinking. I consider chaos a gift."
—Septima Poinsette Clark

In the spring of 1973, black feminist writer Doris Wright called a meeting to discuss "Black Women and Their Relationship to the Women's Movement." What followed was the formation of the National Black Feminist Organization (NFBO). The group was founded to address unique issues faced by black women in America. The civil rights movement in the1950s and 1960s were crucial in the fight for equality among American blacks, and the women's movement prompted earlier in the century had already taken a strong stance. While both movements sought equality for all women and all races, the specific situation of black women in America needed to be recognized, and their concerns directly identified and managed these issues.

Black women found that in the Civil Rights movement, their roles were downplayed, ignored, or even challenged, while within the women's movement, they faced the same discrimination they fought against with the Civil Rights movement. Brenda Eichelberger illuminates these difficulties in an undated interview:

"I didn't know any other black woman felt the way that I did about feminism. I knew white women who were my friends, but they didn't have the added oppression of race. A lot of black groups were macho. I couldn't completely identify with any group. Anyway, all I need to know was that one woman anywhere who felt like I did." (Secret Storm, 1975).

The NFBO stopped working on a national level in 1977, but the movement prompted the creation of other independent outlets for black women seeking unity and a voice in the community. What we find in the following letters are examples of such situations, women who are caught in a quandary, fused into a society concerned with both civil rights and feminism, but living with an uncomfortable feeling of being trodden upon in both areas.

"I was black growing up in an all-white neighborhood, so I felt like I just didn't fit in. I felt like I wasn't as good as everybody."—Nakia, age 27

Social rejection based on physical appearance is painful at any age, but it is especially hard on young girls of color. Young girls are highly attuned to the nuances of physical attractiveness. They are much more sensitive to the social importance of good looks, including skin color. Above, Nakia states this simply. Stephanie recounts a more telling story of how she acknowledged the beauty in her body and her more ethnic physical traits. She was already a strong woman at a young age. She loved her physical appearance, yet it was a parent's off-handed comment that brought her to a realization about her weight that she hasn't forgotten to this day. It wasn't until she was in her twenties that Stephanie was finally able to cope with this insecurity:

"Growing up black in a mostly white town is hard, and finding your identity because of that can be even more difficult. I just want you to know that no matter what color your skin is, that you are beautiful. Don't worry that your hair isn't as long or as straight as all of your friends. Don't worry that you're a little bit 'thicker' than everyone else; you're amazing. Don't let people dumb you down. Don't let your black friends tell you that you're 'too white' for speaking proper English. Just be you.

My self-esteem or lack thereof, started nearly a half a century ago. I remember like it was yesterday. My mom took me shopping for school clothes. I was getting ready to start first grade and clothes didn't fit me like they did other girls. I was basically as wide as I was tall. I had been that way since birth, but didn't know it until that day! My mom and I returned home from shopping and I was so excited to have new clothes. My mom told me to try on my new clothes and show them to my dad. I put on my red stretch pants and matching top. I was so proud and feeling so good.

In a matter of seconds, with one comment, my spirit was crushed. My dad said, 'Jesus Christ! You look like the side of a barn!' I was so embarrassed, and remember that feeling even though it was all those years ago, because I knew that the side of a barn wasn't a good thing!

From that day on, I never liked the color red and never wore it again. All my life I heard 'Stephanie's so pretty, but...' For some reason, I always blocked out the 'but' until that day. Now, my dad was a 'big' man, but that was ok for him because he was a man who played football. I immediately went into a shy, self-conscious mode until my late 20s." —Stephanie, age 40

Diane writes about the difficulties she faced as an intellectual and a woman, and how ignorance and stereotypical attitudes about race and gender seemed to undermine her natural capabilities when she was determined to set herself apart. Her frustrations came out in anger, and it took time and experience to transform her anger into more manageable and positive coping strategies:

"When I was younger, I faced grave adversity in the likes of what amounted to attacks against my gender, my race, and my intellect. For example, I often felt resistance to my ideas and my skills from individuals who seemed to dislike that I could do things that were considered UN-traditional for a woman. I often experienced the ignorance of racism from co-workers and collegiate classmates who assumed (based on no real fact or information) that because I am African-American, I therefore must be defaulted into a subpar category of inability, insufficiency, and ineptitude.

At first, I confronted this ignorance with anger and hostility, often belittling myself to the minimal level of the minds of those who were oppressing me. However, as I have grown, I have learned that I am powerful and capable. I can now hold my peace, resist the pressure to belittle my strengths and my skills in order to fit into this miniature box others have of where I am 'supposed to' belong, and I rely upon my faith in a God— who can do far more than anything I can imagine! As a result, I have overcome these adversities.

What I learned that I carry with me today is that I can be and I can do whatever I can imagine. Individuals who are incapable of understanding that will always resist what they do not understand. Those who are threatened respond to me from a place of insecurity and fear because they don't possess the courage and the integrity to trust my vision or my spirit. It's okay that they resist me. What is not okay is for me to reduce my strengths, to belittle my abilities, or negate my intellect in order to appease their insecurities. I know now to trust myself and to believe in the voice from within that says, 'Yes, I can!'"—Diane, age 40

2 Being an Immigrant

"Nobody can make you feel inferior without your consent."
—Eleanor Roosevelt

In the process of selecting women to contribute to this work, I spoke with many women who are immigrants to this country. They commonly described that as children and adolescents, they perceived mainstream America as unwelcoming and even disparaging. Additionally, their desire to assimilate was frequently met with resistance from their first-generation parents. Basic rites of passage such as dating, expressions of sexual attraction, and social interactions outside of school become battlegrounds for immigrant families, and a source for strained family dynamics. Also, a resistance to assimilation can build when parents force their children to embrace the new culture, and attempt to be more American.

I remember the story told to me by a friend of mine with immigrant ancestors, who moved from Italy at the turn of the century. Their father, Giuseppe, had been a poor farmer his entire life. In desperation, he followed his brothers to America, and eventually settled in Chicago. Due to his low social status in Italy, he refused to allow his family to speak the language or to follow many Italian customs. By the third generation, an entire family of Italians did not know how to speak Italian. While Italian foods were still common at family gatherings, much more of the family's traditions and culture was lost. It wasn't until the third and fourth generations that the family proactively sought to regain their ethnic background.

A typical scenario, however, is one where first generation immigrants cling staunchly to their heritage while their children seek to fit into the new society by disguising their non-American background. I recall another friend who was born in the Caribbean and migrated to the U.S. at a very young age. Her parents strongly resisted her attempts to assimilate into the American culture. This caused stress in their relationship, particularly during the adolescent years, a time when she was most vulnerable to negative social influences. The emotional impact was long lasting.

First- and second-generation immigrants Michelle, Carolina, and Bianca share their personal experiences:

"I wished I was American; I renounced every part of my cultural heritage to fit in. I developed an identity crisis; who was I? It wasn't until my twenties that I learned to embrace my culture, to incorporate it into my identity as an American, and by becoming bi-cultural, felt whole."—Michelle, age 38

While Michelle renounced her heritage, Carolina attempted to balance her life between her parents' wishes and her own independence. In a country with more freedoms available than in her native Mexico, Carolina realized she couldn't limit herself to her parents' parameters of social conduct and family life. She stepped away from cultural expectations while maintaining a personal connection to her heritage.

"I'm a first generation Mexican-American, and eldest child to two Mexican immigrants living in Chicago. My parents were very traditional in their ways, and they were much older than my friends' parents. Not only there was a generation gap, but also a major cultural gap.

My father knew that I was a good student, but he did not know that I had much more ambition. When I had informed him that I would move to Urbana, IL, a three hour trip from Chicago, the news infuriated him. He had never imaged that I would want to leave home. He honestly thought that I after high school I would be a cashier at one of the major grocery stores in the neighborhood. We ended up having an all-out shouting match, with me saying that I will [sic] leave with or without his blessing, and with him saying that he would dictate what my future would be.

Lots of tears rolled down my face because I never thought that my father would not want me to be more. I have always been told that the reason that immigrants come to the USA is to work, and to provide their children an education and opportunities that they never had; for their kids to have a better future, and to get away from the low paying job. For him to react in such a negative way confused me. I learned from my mom that it was fear that prompted my dad's negative reaction to my college announcement. He feared what the outside world would do to me. I basically had a sheltered life: school, books, very few friends, no dating allowed, no extracurricular activities, and no extended family. By leaving home, I would be fair game to the outside world. Neither he nor mom would be there to protect me.

I was humbled that they loved me so much. I had to assure both of them that they had taught me well what is

[sic] expected of me. Temptations will [sic] come, of course, but I would prevail." —Carolina, age 30

Bianca made the assumption that her parents were against her, and did not understand who she was or what she was going through. This is common in many cultures as teens try to make their own imprint on the world. This stubborn insistence on rebellion and alienation is thought to be a mixture of biological and behavioral, as the front lobe of the brain, which makes sense of others' motives and viewpoints, hasn't fully developed. At this age, young adults have the intelligence to think and behave as they wish. Although they have the ability to think through their actions, their ability to think further into the outcome of their actions seems is only partly developed. As we look at Bianca, it is clear she felt the same way many of us did, that our parents obviously didn't know what we were going through.

"As a teen/young lady, we do not realize this. We assume the world, our parents, are all against us...plus coming here to Chicago was pretty tough already, having to learn the language and attend a new school and all, especially when you know no English. Believe me, I learned quickly with the help of my cousin. We made a pact: I will teach you Spanish, you teach me English. Even as a teen I did networking (LOL). Looking back, it isn't, or wasn't, like that at all. I remember coming from a happy place where both parents were present, and I had the best always. My mom took good care of us, and my dad had a great job and he supported us well."—Bianca, age 27

3 Familial Adversity

"Trouble is a part of your life, and if you don't share it, you don't give the person who loves you a chance to love you enough."
—Dinah Shore

Traversing the boundaries of racial and ethnic backgrounds, many young women are burdened with environmental stressors such as domestic violence, troubled parents, sexual abuse, divorce, or medical illness. The following stories demonstrate how women who face these problems overcame adversity, and how resilience and positive self-esteem helped them not only survive, but thrive. By subscribing to a broader value system, they are able to navigate through the most difficult and challenging life circumstances.

"At times you have doubted your ability, but that only pressed you to push harder. There are those who believe you should be a statistic, growing up in a modern-day project, the product of a single-parent home. What was not accounted for was the community and extended family that embraced you, making it mandatory for you to believe in yourself."—Keely, age 40

Kate overcame an enormous amount of adversity when divorce separated her from her father. Sexual molestation at a young age from her mother's boyfriends left her with few places to turn to, yet as you can see, she found a way to manage that pain. She used her spiritual beliefs to transform herself into a well-rounded person with an ability to adjust to a variety of seemingly impossible situations.

"It all came to an end when my dad and mom separated, which devastated me the most since I was the oldest. Having my dad out of my life was very emotional, and maybe I expressed it by being a little shy and withdrawn. Family issues were pretty much swept under the rug, and life continued. The women in my family were strong and happy. They taught me that no matter what, you celebrate life. I held on to the memories; they got me through a lot, and I focused and did well in school, and helped my mom.

My mom dated for awhile, and she did the best she could. I was growing and going through the changes of life, and [a couple of her boyfriends] had tried to molest me, as in touching me and making me feel very uncomfortable, which is terrible for any young girl to go through, and feel like it's her fault. What got me through those years was again God's presence, and my grandmother, who always loved me. Not that my mom didn't, but there was a special kind of love from my grandma that made me feel like no one can [sic] break through. I had and have some amazing uncles that I loved dearly; they also taught me that there are good men out there, and that you give yourself respect, no matter what, and always be a lady. The negative forces that I encountered made me stronger. At the time I did not know, but in my heart I felt that one day it would all be worth the ride.

Take care of yourself. Love yourself. Love those around
you, and let go of things that keep you down. Pray, keep
the Lord close to you, and your family as well. We must
create a healthy relationship with ourselves first, beginning
with our internal self, and that will resonate to our external
self...allowing for peace, balance and harmony."
—Kate, age 28

Adversity comes in many forms. Like Kate, many writers
describe dealing with situations beyond their control.
Adults may be either unwilling or incapable of intervening
in a situation. For better or worse, a young woman who
seeks to take control of a situation like this often affixes
herself with blame in the process of trying to understand
the actions of those around her. In another letter, Joann
talks about her struggles growing up with a mother
suffering from mental illness.

"I love you. I know it is a little hard to believe right now
since you are having a hard time loving yourself, but I do
love you. I know there are things that feel completely
overwhelming right now; your mom's constant physical
pain and depression, your sister's leaving for college, and
therefore leaving you, the abuse you are enduring from a
boy in your life. It is all making you feel like you are alone
and cold and small. There are days when all you can do is
sit on your bed and trace the flowers on your comforter
while feel your skin warmed by the sunlight coming
through the window. It feels like you are being wrapped in
a hug.

There are days when it feels like no one, not even you,
understands why all this is happening and you just want to
know how you can stop it and feel like a "normal" kid with
a normal, happy family. A normal family has a healthy
mom, and a dad who lives with you, and Sunday dinners at
grandma's house, and enough money to buy the good

cereal every day, not just for your birthday. You sit and think that there MUST be something wrong with you that causes your mom's mood swings. You sit and think YOU must have done something wrong, broken a bunch of secret rules that are written in a secret book, secret rules that you are now being punished for breaking.

So you write. You write in your journal every chance you get. You write poem after poem after poem. You keep that journal with you everywhere you go. It is a way to get out everything that you are feeling. It is a way to talk about all the things that are making you hurt, all the ways that people are hurting you. You write and you study.

That new history teacher, she is a blessing to you because she understands that you and your classmates need to think and have opinions. That new history teacher is strict and proper. She wears a blazer and heels to school every day. Her voice fills the room. That new history teacher is giving you permission to be smart. She is giving you permission to be horrible at softball. She asks you "why" questions that don't have a clear cut answer. She wants to help you. She isn't the only one. Others will help you too.

Own your gifts, find people who appreciate you. Speak. Keep writing in your journal. Keep being curious and keep questioning everything. You will find people and communities who value that. Keep learning. Keep praying. God is listening. Dealing with your mom's depression has made you a fantastic listener; that is a gift. It has given you such compassion. Your thirst for knowledge will allow you to surround yourself with smart people with unique gifts, and you will help them realize their potential. And then you will realize your OWN potential."—Joann, age 35

Sometimes adults neglect to fully grasp the value their

mere presence has on a young woman. Natalie discusses growing up without her father, and how his absence in her life left her feeling defeated.

"You've had many reasons—and justifiable ones—to give up and remain defeated by your many obstacles in life, the first being raised without your father. I realize how difficult it was for you and your mother to manage alone in a time where it wasn't accepted for a white woman to have a black child, and without the support and protection of your father. It is understandable to feel a lack of identity, a fear of acceptance and confusion about where you fit in life."—Natalie, age 30

As Veronica grew up, she struggled with family strife, including an absent parent and considerable economic challenges:

"Your mother was filled with fear while raising three girls on her own, and your father was so conflicted between leaving his girls and staying with her, [so] your life was in a perpetual emotional chaos. They finally split when you were five years old, [and] she pined for him endlessly as he drifted in and out of your lives. Thank God for the huge family your mother had, and [your] amazing grandparents that lived two doors down.

You endured discrimination from the Greek side of your family because you were not 100%. You endured discrimination by being bused into inner city schools during the early 70's. You learned that skin and beauty do not determine a lovely human soul, [and] that being cute has its advantages, but learning how to be beautiful within takes work and forgiveness.

These forces made up your early childhood existence, and became an unconscious pattern you would play out in love relationships for years to come—forever choosing men that were unavailable to you because the pushing, pulling, and pining pain felt so familiar to you...it felt like home. My advice is to navigate your life with poise, charm, and indomitable spirit."—Veronica, age 42

Assignment#2: The previous section of this book contains letters which explore the transitional phase from youth to early adulthood. If you are an adult woman, discuss one unplanned life change that you went through which has impacted your life for the better. If you have yet to reach this cusp as a young woman, instead consider one goal, ambition, or achievement which you feel will mark the beginning of this stage in your life's journey.

SANKARSINGH

A LOVE LETTER TO ME

PART III
DEVELOPMENT OF THE SELF

1 Adulthood

"What is an adult? A child blown up by age."
—Simone de Beauvoir

In the earliest phase of adulthood, we transition from the rigors of discipline at home to the steep learning curve of being on our own, whether at college or in our first apartment away from our parents. This is the beginning of a cusp. Many women will use their past experiences for positive growth, yet others will allow their previous situations to pull them deeper into a state of depression. Thankfully, who you were in high school does not have to be who you are as an adult. You can move from a life where hurtful words and physical appearance keep you on constant edge, to a life founded on establishing an independent personal and social identity, and an internal sense of self -worth. As Mellissa explains in the next letter, you learn about yourself in a more meaningful and lasting way; you begin to discover what you really want in life, and take steps and make changes to achieve it.

"While in college, you lose your Grandmother and are devastated. HOWEVER, you handle it much better than when your mom died. You manage to get straight A's in her honor. You look at the semester you partied too much and your GPA fell, [and] you realize you owe your mother and grandmother an Honor Cord at graduation, and the ability to graduate Summa cum Laude. You push through and you do it. You become Student Government Association Chief Justice, President of the NAACP, President of the Urban Studies Association; you follow your mother's footsteps and pledge Alpha Kappa Alpha, and you tutor elementary students every week. You give back and socialize and you learn to make good grades.

While in college you fall in love with the City. How it runs, how it is built, how do traffic lights take? You realize this is a major. People get paid to do it. Who knew? You major in Urban Studies, then go on to graduate school and earn a Master's in Urban and Regional Planning.

The road is never easy. You are prone to coming up with excuses for everything. At some point you realize being raised in a single [parent] home has absolutely nothing to do with your not going to class when you are at school all day. You realize that many people who have it much worse than you are accomplishing all that you have and more, and don't have all the support you have. You realize you owe it to all who have [sacrificed] and are sacrificing to make sure you have everything you need, [and] most things you want. You owe it to them, and most importantly to yourself, to step up to the plate and be all you can be."
—Melissa, age 27

In some cases, the traumas experienced in adolescence are not simple to overcome. New ideas and situations may further complicate or exacerbate already existent problems. The majority of the writers describe experiencing substantial shifts in their identities and self-concepts as they arrive at the next stage of development, but the transition into adulthood can be difficult, a struggle to move from insecurity to the realization that you are not the only one to live through these experiences. The road to achieving a fulfilling life can be a long and complicated one, with as many missteps as successes, as evidenced in the following letters:

"In my late 20s, I was feeling so desperate; I tried every diet known to man with no success. I got to the point of not wanting to live anymore, and thank God I was able to fight that feeling and made the decision to have gastric bypass surgery to lose the weight. I lost 100 pounds in six months. Since then, I have battled the ups and downs of weight gain and loss, [and] as I get older, I maintain a different outlook on the subject. A few pounds up or down don't affect my self-image like they used to, but I swore to never get 'out of control' again." —Dana, age 38

Strength manifests in different ways. For some, this means succeeding despite the odds, while others derive a sense of accomplishment from knowing when to change course in the pursuit of fresh ideas. Coming to terms with a disease that initially destroyed her focus and changed her educational and career goals, Mary learns to use spirituality to heal and improve herself, setting aside her original ambitions and finding deeper fulfillment in her new life.

"When I was diagnosed with ulcerative colitis, my dreams of becoming an English literature professor were replaced with a lifelong search for health, happiness, and spiritual awareness. The road was not always smooth. Each medical challenge and surgery made the journey of becoming a wellness educator and president of my company, Target Health Systems, Inc., that much more difficult, that much more urgent. The personal challenges—surviving my divorces and coming to terms with the 'rules' I had stubbornly adopted to be the perfect 'everything'—made the journey of becoming a

compassionate, but assertive woman more necessary.
The dichotomy between the masculine and feminine roles,
as I saw them, became more confusing. Was I the
'masculine' persona of my creative father/entrepreneur, or
the 'feminine' counterpart of my sweet, nurturing mother?
Knowing now that I can be both, I honor whoever I am at
any moment in time…a mom, a warrior, a lover, an
entrepreneur, a woman, a child, an educator, a student of
life, an evolving spirit.   I strive to love them all."
—Mary, age 50

Life after school is full of the unexpected. Even women
who experienced success in their more formative years can
discover their challenges increase when they enter the job
market. Tiffany finds self-admiration in her willingness to
persevere after experiencing the disappointment of a failed
career move.

"I love your tenacity! When you graduated from college
without a dream job waiting, you persevered by returning
to school and choosing a career that would provide
comfortably for you and your son. You excelled in school
and after eight months, you attended a job fair and claimed
a new career. This willpower and determination make me
very proud of you!" —Tiffany, age 28

Maria explains how she chose a self-deprecating life of
rebellion as she sought to uncover and understand her
individual identity. Later in life, she was able to overcome
her naïve behavior and seek wisdom through spirituality.
She was not looking for answers to simply fall into her lap;
she learned from her mistakes, and in the process, she
found the person she'd been praying for.

"My teen years were OK. I was doing well in school (and
finished high school early). I guess I was bored or
rebellious. My head blew up. I started hanging with the

wrong crowd, thought I could just start acting up, getting high, smoking, drinking. It was no one but me who decided that I wanted to run the streets and act a fool, but hey, it was the in thing. I wanted to hang with my friends. I wound up running away, and stayed at my so-called boyfriend's house. He had no love for me. I was young, like I say. It was the kind of love that leaves you empty inside, and you hope that it's going to change, but it doesn't. Well, that did not last long because my mom and MiAmor (grandma) waited patiently for me, and sent me off to Florida one way, so that I could think and learn a lesson. Believe me, I learned my lesson quick.

I came back to Chicago, and calmed down a little. Soon after this, I decided to get married, at 19—God, no!—yes, married. What I thought would be the best decision ever tuned into a nightmare. How could this be? I knew how to cook, clean, work, take care of a home. Imagine—I was 19 and he was 27. I got pregnant a few months into the marriage. He was very manipulative, a cheater, liar, abusive, and also a drug user. I was very naïve. It was no more about me or us; it was about him and the baby. I had lost myself, my spirit, withdrawn (sic) from family and friends. How naïve, thinking that I could change him, that he truly loved me, that by staying, things would get better, that we could work on it. Abusers and drug users do not change unless they choose to. I know that now!

I was in an abusive relationship for the next 14 years. There were plenty of nights where I would cry myself to sleep, thinking and replaying it over and over in my head. Walking on eggshells—what a way to live, huh? (But where will I go, and what am I going to do?) I was ashamed and felt no self-worth. I felt as though I had no choice. I remember him saying clearly one night, 'Who would want you—a woman with kids? No man in his right mind.' I remember saying in my head, 'One day, watch me,' and I prayed, I always prayed, that God would give me the wisdom and the strength to get through it all, and in him I trusted 24/7.

I remember one night I was talking with a friend, and I had thought it out and mentioned [that] if I had a place to go, I swore I would leave. She offered a space—a floor. I looked at her and said, 'Are you for real? With my kids?' She looked at me and said, 'Yes, you can come whenever.' That night, I grabbed my daughters and [ran] down the stairs as fast as I could, telling my babies, 'Run, run!' And I never looked back. Oh yeah, he begged me back, but my inner spirit said, 'No, stay focused...you will be ok,' and that's what I did. The drive, the inner voice would end up helping me empower other women, so I kept going like the little train that could, persistent, protecting my kids. I remember giving thanks, saying to myself 'never again.'

A few years went by, and I met my son's father. He was so handsome and perfect, hardworking—GOD, so good–looking!—good to me and my kids...wow. Never seeing the signs, I fell in love, but grew out of it not too long after we moved in together. I remember the first time he slapped me. It was like going back in time just when I thought life was finally going to be good to me—starting to spread my wings. Wondering what I had done, saying to myself maybe I was wrong. Next time I won't say it that way, or laugh so much, or wear these jeans. I couldn't speak to his friends when we went out—for that I got a fist to the face one night, and just like abusers' clockwork, he apologized. I accepted because he loved me, (or so I thought).

We moved on, had a son together. The abuse got worse—punching, slapping, embarrassed in front of friends. That craziness lasted 10 years. It was a roller coaster ride indeed. He damaged my face so bad one time that I had to hide from my kids for three weeks, and even then I was afraid to press charges. I was humiliated, and I couldn't do it anymore. I was tired and worn out; my spirit was broken; it was the last straw. My mom always was there telling me she would support my choices.

It was a long road. I got out of that relationship, learned lots of lessons, learned to really love me and accept who I was then, and now, and that when someone loves you, they love you unconditionally, and want you to grow and be who you are, and they don't judge you; they love you no matter what, just like I love me. That little shy, chunky Spanish-speaking girl from Puerto Rico finally has spread her wings and said, 'Look at me, see my colors, feel my spirit. I am a child of God, and I am love, and I will continue to grow and nurture those who need nurturing, and spread the word that no one should ever let anyone manipulate her, and that all things are possible under God. Those doors are opening wide, that I am WOMAN, and my mission is to help and empower other young ladies/women, so that they can to be butterflies one day. My dream was to work with battered women and inner city children at risk, and guess what? It is called: BUTTERFLIES IN TRANSITION. It is mine and I own it.

I am living the dream, the impossible. Remember I am a statistic, but I refuse to give up! I remember thinking I needed to be still and it would all come to me, and it did. I will never in my lifetime allow anyone to disrespect me and manipulate me in any shape or form, and I will continue to reach out to other victims, and those who need me to cross that bridge.

Blessed with four children and three grandkids, I am still learning on that great journey. There are many things that I would love to do and see done. For instance [I am now working on] a convention for gay/lesbian teens. So be you so that you can reach out to another and help them on their journey. Always question, and know there are many strong women out there that are willing to help. Please approach us!" —Maria, age 45

For some, early adulthood may entail challenging what others think about us and our abilities. In the next letter, Linda describes her desire and determination to achieve, despite the resistance and lack of interest she perceived from adults. Although she lives in a society that is relatively advanced in regard to women's equality, she nevertheless found discouragement, even in the very institution whose purpose is to encourage young people to succeed.

"Like my fellow senior classmates, I too decided to pursue college even though my high school counselor tried to discourage me, stating that my PSAT scores would not get me into the university of my choice, University of Illinois-Urbana. However, I did fill out a college application. Take note— I only filled out one for the School of Engineering at the University of Illinois. No one told me that I needed to fill out more applications to other universities. My high school counselor was of no use to me. Fortunately, I did get accepted—with a full scholarship." —Linda, age 25

Hiding is negative pattern used to disguise what is really going on in our lives. The following women describe hiding behind a smile or a "helping" personality. They use the joy they bring to others to mask their own pain. They understand who they are and what they are doing. Their efforts to help others may define their outer person, but the person they really are seeks solace away from those they please. They reflect on what they deem as faults. You can probably recognize how they feel, and see how they begin to step out of their skin to reveal who they truly are.

"Our passion was nursing, always wanting to help and care for others. If anyone was in pain, we would be drawn to them like a magnet, wanting to help, love, and comfort...almost as if it was lessening our own pain within. Others seem to appreciate that quality in us, old reliable T, always there for a person in need. Not to be mistaken as a softy, we put up walls and barriers on just how close we would allow others to come into our heart, our thoughts, the whole time secretly and desperately desiring to be loved...remember? It became the norm to do for others, even though the heart said no, letting others take advantage of us until it hurt beyond repair, then [walking] away and never looking back, crossing people out of our life with no communication on why. Burying the pain of the loss in with all the other pain that filled the heart. It was always their fault, we would say; they caused the demise of the relationship.

How often you have tried to hide your sparkly star under a bushel, and 'shrink to fit' to become the person you thought they wanted you to be, just so you could be near them, make it right, fix that hurt from so long ago, and in the present moment no less, as if that is even possible. It does not work that way, and trying to fix the past robs the now of its joy. Something that has already happened cannot be changed; release guilt because it is just another form of fear. Learn how to choose wisely, and be a compassionate warrior."—Erin, age 27

Like Erin, many women find that true maturity and adulthood is about challenging pre-conceived notions about not just the world, but the internal self. Sometimes we think we know who we are, but when we find ourselves under pressure, we come to find greater strengths and abilities than we thought we were capable of. The following letter charts one woman's powerful course of change and self-discovery as she pushes against her own limitations and the safety of what she believes she knows about herself.

"Taking care of strangers, that's what we became the best at! Nursing was something we loved, enjoyed, and looked forward to doing. I begin to think about how, upon college graduation, we only wanted to take care of adults, NO EXCEPTIONS! Children were out of the question; even in hospital rotation we did everything possible to avoid the children. Their sadness hit too close to our own. The vivid images and memories of ourselves spending time in the hospital, starting as young as three, was too painful to be around. Hurtful memories of being the odd kid out came rushing back, and the fear of breaking down, instead of being caring and supportive, kept us away from pediatrics.

Remember those moments of sheer fear as the FIRST nursing job we received was with babies? Remember wanting to turn the job down, but not wanting to explain why? I laugh now when I think about it, I laugh even harder at the fact that that is where we would spend our bedside nursing career, in pediatrics, and completely loving it.

Life was great for years; we successfully tucked away our pain, became a tad better in hiding our insecurities, and thought nothing of not having any self love. Do you remember how we allowed our acceptance and accolades for being a nurse to boost our ego? 'People like me,' 'people love me,' 'people think I'm great' because I'm a nurse and I help them and others. Wow, finally we were loved. So just like anything else, we became aggressive for approval, and felt the need to be the absolute best. Not because we really wanted to be, but because it would keep others loving us.

Hey, do you remember the breakdown? We talked about travel nursing; we knew we needed to grow and change, begin to get to the root of this pain. We knew there was more to us than what we were living. We were slowly beginning to realize that no matter how much love and desperation we forced on others, that we did not love ourself. We knew this, and now we wanted to do something about it.

Remember the day we lay in the middle of the floor in that beautiful apartment in Atlanta, crying so hard that it hurt? Remember how we stopped the process of letting go because it was too overwhelming? Remember all the cigarettes we smoked, all the partying we did, and all the drinks we consumed to push the pain away? Remember all the shopping sprees, spending money we should have saved or paid our bills with? Remember wishing we would die...?

I spent last week thinking about this journey of self-growth and self-love that we ventured out on, and I cried; I cried long, I cried hard. But then I began to smile, laugh, and smile some more, as I think back to the apartment in Boston, after the breakdown in Atlanta. I think about the challenges we faced professionally in Boston, and I remember the night we opened up the lock on the heart and decided to dig in again. Not ready to let go of our self-inflicted crutches, we began to run, one mile, two miles, three miles, all followed by 'well deserved' cigarettes, or so we thought.

But remember how great we felt after running? It became a form of clearing the head, cleansing the soul. Running became our new habit! As we made that move to Chicago in the spring, the unknown no longer scared us. Well, maybe a little; remember being the 'new nurse' yet again? But Boston taught us how attitude and insecurity-laced toughness is not the road to remain on, so we attempted to present a softer version of ourselves. I laugh, because it was so forced.

We would come face to face with ourselves once again in that loft apartment in Old Town, standing in front of that floor length mirror just out of the shower...we stood at that mirror, and looked ourselves in the eye and admitted out loud, 'I don't like you,' 'I don't love you,' 'I would not want you as a best friend.' Remember how the tears would not stop? Remember how we laid down in the fetal position, declaring our utter dislike for each other? The next day on our long run (we were now training for the Chicago Marathon), we ran and cried some more. Twelve miles later, we were still crying as we hit the shower, we were still crying as we exited the shower. Finding ourselves back in front of that full length mirror, we stared at each other again. The tears disappear, we pull on our belly fat, we go in for a close up on the face we have self-labeled 'ugly,' and we stare.

Once again, we repeat the words of dislike and no love aloud, and just as we turn to walk away from each other, we stop, and look each other in the eyes, and say aloud: 'if you don't like me, if you don't love me, if you don't want me as a friend...how the hell can you expect anyone else to have those feelings towards you? Life began to change that evening, really change. We became one; we began to go within, and open wounds.

Completing the marathon gave us the confidence to dig deeper. Yoga seemed to appear out of nowhere during our marathon training, as if it was something we should have been doing all along (we now know that to be true for us). The heart opened more. Remember how our worst enemy, the mirror, became our best friend? How we longed for mirror time so we could look each other in the eyes for strength, peace, and guidance? Remember the day we put the cigarettes down and stopped consuming hard alcohol? Remember how weight began to fall off our body, and how we looked in that mirror and saw the same external beauty that we were now feeling internally?

Remember the day we decided yoga and self-love and awareness [were things] we wanted to share with the world, and how our self-love, trust, and respect for each other allowed us to walk away from that stable nursing income and comfortable life style, to venture out on our heart's desire and live our dream, share our story, and live our life to the fullest? Even if it meant we would need to be a little uncomfortable? Even if it meant we may have to experience fear? I remember.

So here we stand today as one, loving life and loving self. Enjoying this part of life's journey, living our dream, aiming to reach our goals, sharing our desire to teach others how to create a healthy mind, body, and spirit from the internal to the external self. Knowing that in the journey of life, one will experience insecurity, pain, pleasure, love and obstacles...but with self-love, created by a healthy mind, body, and spirit, all can be accomplished! We must create a healthy relationship with ourselves first, beginning with our internal self, and that will resonate to our external self, allowing for Peace, Balance, and Harmony!"—Lauren, age 29

In Lauren's letter and the next as well, we sense a shift away from fear and a downtrodden spirit, to a sense of fulfillment. We see the emphasis these women place, not on who they were, but on who they are at present. There is always hope for tomorrow, even if today was less than satisfactory.

"I love your confidence! In the past, you based your personal value on someone else's love. You felt if a 'significant other' wanted to be with you, then you were worthy. I am overjoyed that your self-esteem has detached from a significant other's love or acceptance. I am happy you are able to observe all of your blessings and appreciate the abundance of love given by all who truly love you unconditionally, especially God."—Lilly, age 23

A new—or renewed—confidence in life starts to take shape in the mid-twenties as we begin to see the small successes that make us beautiful, worthwhile people. We may find relationships with partners who treat us well, and perhaps we learn from those who don't. We also start to define ourselves career-wise and socially, and we set about transforming our dreams into reality. Those quirky traits that defined us as "weird" in high school become advantages as adults, as Valeria describes:

"You have enjoyed being different most of your life. You take into account others' needs and expectations, but when it comes down to it, you don't compromise your integrity or your beliefs for someone else. That is core to who you are, and worthy of respect. You are someone who appreciates the light in others and tries to make it shine. You are generous and loyal, and creative and fun. You enjoy making people laugh, knowing that laughter is sometimes the only way to get a point across, ease a troubled mind or heal a person's tattered soul. You don't look for the easiest route; you look for the most interesting one."—Valeria, age 25

Like Valeria, Sierra's simple message also urges us in a direction of self-worth. She reminds us that there is always a tomorrow, and that we always have time to change.

"Despite the struggles you face year after year, facing life on your own, you hold your head high and with pride every day. Even when you feel defeated, the world still sees you as a confident and secure woman. Please remember that even though times may be rough, there is ALWAYS a tomorrow. The sun will always shine and bring a new day for you to pick yourself up and start all over again—no matter what! Always know that I love you just the way you are."—Sierra, age 27

Nancy celebrates her learning from past experiences, and reaffirms her belief that "settling" is not the answer.

"I am happy that past hurts have not made you bitter. You give yourself time to mend your heart and forgive yourself. It is wonderful that you still believe in real love and refuse to attach your heart to anything less than genuine love...NEVER, EVER SETTLING!"
—Nancy, age 24

The next few letters express triumphs which emerge from perceived failures. As it has been reinforced throughout this book, an instrumental part of life is identifying our past experiences and learning from them. I encourage you to take strength and encouragement from their insights as you recognize that their struggles are not much different from your own.

"Even though you married the wrong man for the wrong reasons, it's ok that it happened. Yes, he cheated; yes, he lied. But he gave you two of the most beautiful children in the world. Compassionate, funny, amazing children that the world would be sorry if they had never been born. Your daughter and your son have the best of you, and the best of him. Don't let who he has become defeat them Show them that they are worthy, even though their father didn't show them that YOU were."—Brenda, age 28

"Be proud of yourself for overcoming obstacles. Deciding to have the gastric lap band surgery was an amazing step. It was scary and unknown, but it was the best thing you possibly could have done for yourself. Look at yourself in the mirror now. Losing over 100 pounds is an accomplishment, not something to be ashamed of. Don't look in the mirror and continue to see all of your flaws...look and see your strengths." —Christine, age 28

"Continue to see the good in people. Don't let past experiences sour you on trust. Be kind, be honest, and be faithful. Remember that you have to take care of you before you can take care of anyone else. Quit martyring yourself and putting yourself last. When that happens, things fall apart and you feel so resentful that it's hard to move forward."—Kelly, age 26

"Take care of yourself. Love yourself. Love those around you; and let go of things that keep you down. Pray, keep the Lord close to you, and your family as well. Don't take people for granted. Be safe, but take risks."
—Wanda, age 29

One tactic many successful women adopt to overcome internal, external, and circumstantial obstacles, is to rely on an inner receptacle of faith and spirituality. No matter what denomination you choose, a spiritual practice imparts a feeling of self-centeredness. The chaos around you will become insignificant in comparison to a higher purpose, and knowing that you are loved despite, and even because of your inadequacies and failures gives you the confidence to reveal your true self.

"Being a 'Fearless Woman' holding the sword draws me to a place of inner strength, filled with a joyful passion for living life to its fullest. My prayer is that every day I will open my heart to love and forgiveness, that I will be mesmerized by the beauty and joy surrounding me, and that I can be grateful for and humbled by the lessons from the messengers God sends me (thank you, dear sons). And, on top of this all, I want to remember and experience that when I giggle, which is not often enough, I feel like there are champagne bubbles coursing through my veins. Life is too beautiful to be too serious and not enjoy every bubble!"— Rianna, age 29

"Fearless Wisdom: Jump fearlessly into the current of God's blessings and be carried joyously to a place of peace, passion, and wonder!"—Hillary, age 29

Strength shows in our inner selves, and can be recognized not only by our individual and personal success, but in the eyes of our children. The following women recognize that they are strong; their letters affirm their deep sense of self-appreciation.

"I love your power! Your roles as head of household and single parent helped shape your self-worth. At an early age, you had to become responsible, mature, and strong. Initially, you felt overwhelmed by the tasks bestowed upon you and at times doubted your abilities. Even now, sometimes you struggle to find balance and [you] make mistakes, but your continued success is evident in the wonderful child you nurture, love, and cherish. He often tells you that you are great mom, and shows you constantly how much he appreciates everything you do for him."
—Wendy, age 28

"We both have to agree, 23 years old was too young for you to marry, but you made the right choice to get married and have your son. And although the marriage wasn't true love, the 20 years taught you many great lessons: God is real; hurt and pain don't last forever; family is more important than work; children are your greatest joy; friendships are your refuge in time of need; and you must always nurture and take care of your body, mind, and spirit."—Nicole, age 44

Many of the letters in the final section of this chapter reveal the comfort of personal affirmation. Statements such as "I love myself" and "I am a beautiful person" are common claims made by the writers. Amazing changes can be realized by simply reasserting that you are valuable not only to yourself, but to those around you. These women found a sense of personal power in creating positive messages which promote self-awareness. Strength may be gleaned by following the affirmations they applied to themselves.

"I want to let you know that you are wonderful and I would not change you for the world. You are an example to your friends, family, peers and colleagues! I appreciate you so much. You inspire me to do better and grow more. Your perseverance is so encouraging to me and you make me feel like there is nothing I can't do. Stay strong, stay loving, stay beautiful inside. I love you for who you are!"—Zena, age 24

"I love that you know how to upgrade! In the past, because you hated being alone, you dated and befriended people who did not deserve your energy. While the core of you remains unaltered, when dissatisfied, you put in the work to transform. Long ago you deemed your happiness as your own responsibility, therefore you constantly invest and reinvent yourself into the woman you like being. Since fashioning yourself into someone you love, 'me time' is a guilty pleasure you indulge in regularly."
—Francine, age 23

"You are a riddle wrapped in a mystery inside an enigma.

You live a life that interests you, provides you with self-sufficiency, and teaches you much along the way. Though others may say your road is winding, you know that it goes exactly where it needs to take you. You have taken the road less traveled more because that has been what appeals to you than because of some grand design or plan. And yet there has been, in its own way, a plan for your life that is now beginning to be realized. It's taken a long time, and a lot of learning along the way. But you are resilient, you know how to take the right risks, and get up when you fall. There is no growth without failure."—Noel, age 29

"You are beautiful, sexy, a great companion and lover. You would make a great girlfriend and wife. You know this, but this is where you tend to lose faith and get sad. It's OK to go through these emotions, but let me remind you that there is no need for this. Let me remind you that there is a special and perfect plan for your life. God has simply not revealed it to you yet. Despite the divorce four years ago, and despite the break-up with the love of your life earlier this year, you are still a wonderful woman.

These two men were simply not ready to be with you because of their own issues. It is far from anything having to do with you. You know this. These two men broke you to pieces, but because of your wonderful qualities, you picked yourself up and managed to mend your broken heart by doing what was healthy for you. You surrounded yourself with people who love and value you and you believed in yourself. And what's so beautiful about you is that you've been able to forgive and not become bitter toward men and relationships. The fact that you are willing to start over and give the next man a clean and open heart is just an aspect of the person you are. You needed to go through these learning yet terribly difficult situations to prepare you for the next encounter."
—Kathy, age 29

"How quickly it all gets out of balance and how vital your sense of self is to staying in balance. Love yourself! Mental discipline is vital. Our egos are amazing manipulators of our own happiness! Our minds are so powerful, and we take them for granted, letting them drift off to any insane, fear-filled thought [they want] to latch on to, and spin out our life's nightmare from there.

Living a love-filled, fearless life is the only one worth living. Everything else is counterfeit. So go ahead and take a chance. Step up to the plate. Strike out and then step up again. You fall down, you get up.

I love that you have done something that you fear every few years to keep your edge and remind yourself that fear truly is False Evidence Appearing Real. Nothing can hurt you, unless you give it permission to!" —Lana, age 30

2 Midlife

"One of the signs of passing youth is the birth of a sense of fellowship with other human beings as we take our place among them."
—Virginia Woolf

Mid-life. What have we learned since recovering from adolescence, where we were first teased by others, or identified some of our physical and emotional handicaps? In our twenties, we began to address those things that once marred our lives and overwhelmed us. We discovered ourselves. We figured out how to cope with what we saw as insecurities, and used those same imperfections to make our lives better. We dug deep into our souls and found small successes. We learned much about the world, and how the things that troubled us in high school really meant very little.

Now we've hit our thirties and moved beyond. We are strong and confident, and we start to recognize patterns as they emerge, for better or for worse. Our lifelong search to fulfill our dreams is now a reality, in one form or another. What we expected may not have happened, but we realize there is a reason for that. We grew up, we became stronger, and what mattered so much before doesn't seem to be as important as it was then. We begin to cherish the simpler things in life.

The following letters were written by women as they moved into their prime, increasing in self-awareness and confidence, and acquiring a better understanding of themselves. Not only do they appreciate their lived experiences, but they are able to gather wisdom from their past mistakes and gain momentum from their triumphs, both of which act to propel them further along their journey. The amount of pride and self-respect they show as mature adults is a testament to the healing abilities of time, spirituality, and inner reflection.

As you read these letters, imagine yourself in their place 10, 20, even 40 years from now. No matter where you are in life or what you are feeling at the moment, these writers illustrate that attaining such harmony is possible.

"This is your new challenge--making your life your own. Now that you are divorced and raising one child in college, a senior in high school, and an eight-year-old daughter, you must take your life by the reins. You have yet another opportunity to experience an even happier life and make all your dreams come true. You can do it! And be reminded, you are smart, a hard worker, a loving parent, and a loyal friend, and you always choose what is good and true. Keep going for it!"—Monique, age 39

"Those who don't know their history are bound to repeat it. As women in their twenties and thirties take on the roles of wife and mother, we must remember that the quest for gender equality isn't just a women's issue. Those of us who want husbands who will share the joys and burdens of care giving must fight against restrictive ideas of masculinity and femininity that hold both genders back."—Bethany, age 38

"You believe the meaning of life is to make the world better for your having been in it, to leave it better than it was before you. You keep in mind the actions you take every day, and think not just about yourself and what you will get, but how your actions will affect others. First you listen, then you are heard. First you seek to understand, then you are understood. Your goal in every interaction is to add value, or at least pleasure, to those with whom you interact. Your life is filled with love because you are willing to give it freely to those who need it most. You know there is not an unlimited supply of kindness and you share it with everyone you can.

When your days in this life are numbered, you will measure your success by those you have touched, those who love you, and those whose lives have been made better because of knowing you. There's no need for you to be on the front page, no need to be a superstar to many. So long as you have been a superstar to someone, your life will have been well lived."—Jenna, age 41

"These days, I find that there are a lot of things I love about you. However, the ones that come to mind are as follows: your persistence to seek and follow God's plan for your life, your unwillingness to settle for anything below what you're worth, your commitment to the communities in which you work and live, and your faithfulness to your family. As you continue to embark on this next phase of your journey of self-discovery, remember to live like it's your last day, love harder than you ever thought you could, and be humble for all the blessings you are sure to receive!"—Liz, age 43

"This letter is to inform you how much I appreciate you. I've known you my whole life, but it really wasn't until you entered your prime thirties when I [got to know] who you

really are and what you are made of. I can say that I am
nothing but impressed with so many of your qualities, and
I want to let you know why:

You are a loving individual. You are a great friend. Both
men and woman love you and feel loved by you. Your
ability to empathize with people and welcome them into
your life is a quality that I truly admire about you. You are
the type that doesn't make anyone feel left out, and you
have touched so many people because of this. The way
that you give of yourself to people is something that you
should never lose. I don't even think it comes to you as an
effort. It simply is natural to you. You are blessed for
having this quality. You love the family that God has
placed you in. You especially love the children in your
family and you appreciate and take care of your parents.
You enjoy your siblings and are willing to stand by them
through thick and thin.

You are a driven and hard-working individual. You love a
challenge and hard work does not scare you. As a matter
of fact, you have fun with it. You enjoy coming home
from a long day's work and feel like you've accomplished
your goals for the day. Yet you don't take it too seriously,
and you don't let yourself get lost in work. You are able to
leave work at work, and not think about it when it's time
for other things. Of course you worry about the business,
and you have your moments of freak-outs with finances,
but you always find a way of letting go, knowing that God
is on your side to take care of things that are out of your
control. Because of this, you're a talented and successful
business owner!

You are happy, fun, and welcoming, and you love putting a
smile on people's faces, whether it's by being silly, or doing
something funny, or telling a funny story; people love
hanging with you. People want to be around you, and you

too enjoy being around happy people. I think this is why you've been so successful in your business. You are able to create an environment of trust and comfort for your clients so that they continue to come to you and send you business. They know that you have their best interest in mind, and they feel protected and taken care of by you.

You are a woman of faith. You know that you would not be here without God and every single blessing He has given you. Because of this, you don't worry about life too much. You've learned the hard way that when you do worry, you are not putting your faith in God, and you only drive yourself crazy. You are not perfect at this, but wise enough to know when you are not being faithful, and willing to change when you see it.

Jayne, I want to let you know that you are wonderful and I would not change you for the world. You are an example to your friends, family, peers and colleagues. You inspire me to do better and grow more. You're perseverance is so encouraging to me and you make me feel like there is nothing I can't do. Stay strong, stay loving, stay beautiful inside! I love you for who you are."—Jayne, age 39

"Now at 50, you have finally figured it out. It is not about them, it is not about the drama/adrenaline rush. It never has been. It has, and always will be, about your soul's evolution. We each are on our path, and on our way back home to Love. The joy you bring to the world around you is what makes the difference. The magical awareness occurs by staying in the moment, being present, seeing what is front of you, not the illusion you would love to see, or a past wrong you are trying to correct."
—Audrina, age 50

"Everything on this planet called Earth is temporary. Good, happy times or prosperity do not last any more than bad, sad times and those of scarcity. There is birth and death, and in between, life! So live it! It is short and precious. Forgive…and often, for every unkind, angry, guilty, attacking thought you think about yourself.

Be kind to yourself, do not judge yourself so harshly, or doubt yourself with so much vigor, lest you become paralyzed! When you stop judging, beating, hating, angry thoughts, your inner world becomes a quiet, more peaceful place, and then naturally your outer world will as well….Smile often and at strangers; you might just make someone's day. And don't be dismayed if they do not smile back. It wasn't about them anyway. Giving without expectation is one of the amazing keys to happiness and peace. You rock!"—Christy, age 50

"As I look back on my 62 years, I feel so blessed to be where I am, having the guidance to paint the dreams of my future! I am on my path, a continual, sacred journey of learning as much as I can. I, in turn, teach as well as I can. I share with others the options for living happy, healthy, and financially and spiritually abundant lives. Fear ignites action to reach far beyond what we ever thought possible, to step outside the box, to say, 'I can do this!' I am a better person because of this. I believe that challenges are God's way of creating miracles."—Barbara, age 62

3 Achievement

"Optimism is the faith that leads to achievement. Nothing can be done without hope and confidence."
—Helen Keller

All of the women you have read about throughout this book overcame adversity great and small, and offer insight on how they accomplished this. A consensus among the women who wrote about their adolescence is that the best way for a young girl to sustain a sense of confidence is to acquire and demonstrate competence in a given area. These women found that self-confidence emerged with successful skill development and learning. Some experienced success through sports, some in theatre, and others in academia, or in some aspect of their social or personal lives. Many found limited support in the traditional education system. When teachers and counselors didn't provide the same quality of academic advisement as they did to their male counterparts, some women sought out mentors who could help them set and reach meaningful goals. In this manner, success was achieved more often than not, with added determination and discipline.

Often, when we read a magazine or watch television, we see a world of celebrity that appears to us as unreal as make-believe. We see beautiful people on the screen, and don't stop to realize the trials they had to endure in order to achieve the status they found. Step back for a moment to the early 1990s, where a woman sat in a café, using her foot to rock the baby stroller as she sipped on coffee. She jotted notes on napkins. She had no job, an ex-husband, and was homeless and living with friends. She started writing a book in 1990, and through all her personal ordeals, she maintained an active interest in finishing her book.

She suffered through twelve rejections from publishers before a small London press decided to take a chance on the unusual book, and even then the editor at Bloomsbury advised her "to get a day job," as they did not feel she would ever make much money as an author. The book was eventually published in 1997, with a first print of 1000 copies, 500 of which were sent to libraries. A published book is a success in itself, but it was J. K. Rowling's determination and perseverance that turned her simple back-of-a-napkin book into one of the strongest brands in the world. She is currently the most successful writer of all time, and the second wealthiest self-made female billionaire in the world, behind only Oprah Winfrey.

"I always thought about a career, but I was taught that my main role would be wife and mother. I spent my high school days in fantasy, particularly about boys, popularity, marriage, and love. I had little direction in discovering my talents and using that as a career guide." —Rachel, age 34

Rowling's biography illustrates that it's never too late to uncover hidden talents, and take advantage of your own natural gifts. Tracy, another writer, encourages diversity through learning, and advocates taking the challenges of life as fuel to propel you along:

"One thing that I would encourage you [to do is to explore any] subjects that may be of interest to you. I took English literature and philosophy classes along with my science and math courses. I was very aware that I was losing interest in engineering. There is so much pressure for you to choose a major and to stick to it. Yes, I know that I could have made much more money as an electrical engineer but I would not have been happy. Remember that this is your life, not your parents', who may be disappointed in your choices, but it is your future.

You cannot avoid adversity. Face it, explore your possibilities, talk to people (college advisors, professors, peers, parents, etc.); give yourself options. Your future is what you make of it."—Tracy, age 32

Across much of the world, a new equality is dawning. Women's roles have shifted dramatically in the last fifty years: mother, partner, and career woman— these options are now attainable for most women in the western world. Yet women still face the expectation, imposed either externally or by their own deepest patterns of indoctrination, that their only purpose in life is to be a devoted mother and wife, the backdrop to someone else's starring role. Obstacles still exist, and as we have seen through these letters, these obstacles are more common than some would like to believe. Women who found themselves cast in supporting roles transcended them, and it is my hope that by understanding how they broke free and achieved fulfillment, that you too may find your trajectory.

Assignment#3: The final section of this book is given over to letters written by women who are in their life's' prime. If you have already reached this stage in life, take these few pages to think about what your trajectory or plan is for your future years, and where your path has led you. How does it differ from what your young self wanted? What aspects of your past do you feel were the most challenging? What is the one thing in your life about which you are most proud?

If you are younger, try writing a letter to your future self. What questions do you have about your current life or situation which you feel your future self might be able to answer?

SANKARSINGH

A LOVE LETTER TO ME

SUMMARY

The women who have written these pages took time to reflect on who they are and where they came from, surpassing both preconceived notions of gender and identity to succeed in the face of seemingly insurmountable obstacles. They have been plagued with all the complications of youth, from personal issues like acne and weight problems, to social issues brought on by family, friends, and even strangers. Most heartfelt to me were the number of women dealing with sexual abuse. The trauma of being abused even once can scar someone for life. Situations of this sort impact millions of women throughout the US and over the world, but my deepest thanks goes to the brave women who opened their lives to us to better help us understand our own.

Life is a cycle, constantly growing and evolving. Each stepping stone directs us on a new path, where we have the chance to shed our outer shells and create new lives. While we struggle to strengthen our egos through our teenage years, we find later that we cannot experience full spiritual growth without shrinking the same self-centeredness which at one point insulated us from the outside world.   You have seen it in these letters and it has been echoed in the commentary, that the way to inner harmony is to seek personal development in all stages of life.

We find that many of the women on these pages experienced growth by helping others. Some find their own personal growth coincides with their children and family, while others choose to help strangers overcome their own weaknesses as a means of understanding their own situations. Other writers overcame sexism and racism, sometimes together. They grew to have faith in who they became. While problems existed in each one of these women's lives, each found a way to turn struggle into strength. I hope that as you've read these letters, you felt the love that each woman has developed for themselves and for others, as a proud spirit within. As a result, I hope you will see how strong you truly are.

As I was finishing this project, a letter came in from Deanna. Her story encompasses many of the themes we've discussed. She experienced both bullying and sexual molestation as a child, and grew up in a single-parent household, without a father. Like many women all over the world, Deanna was forced to experience abuse and betrayal. Yet she managed to overcome by find ways to demonstrate her resilient spirit. She writes this letter to remind herself of the pain she's been through, and as we've discussed before, she reaffirms that strength through positivity and takes pride in who she is today.

I leave you with Deanna's letter. Remember who you are, and let the journeys of these women remind you that you are special:

"Hi Deanna,

I just wanted to let you know how really proud I am of you. The truth is, I know you have been through a lot in your life, and you have overcome some huge obstacles. No, you were not the prettiest; no, you were not the smartest; and no, you did not grow up with a silver spoon in your mouth. But one thing that I commend you for having is heart.

Deanna, you had the heart to accept that adversity has

been part of your life, and instead of acting as a victim, you became victorious. I know life was not easy for you, growing up in a single-parent household in one of the roughest, drug-infested areas in the Bronx. But you did not let that stop you.

I know growing up with a teenaged mom had to have been difficult. Your mother was a child raising a child. But look at you now. Your mother did the best she could with what she had to raise you and your three siblings. I know not having your dad in your life left you wondering what a real man was like. But God became the Dad you never had. I know being sexually molested left you feeling like all men were dogs...but you have been blessed with a husband and three beautiful daughters.

I know that on your journey to discovering you, you've met some good people and some who did not mean you any good. The truth is, you have learned from both. You've learned to surround yourself with those who wanted something out of life, and for those who didn't, you let them go. You also learned that the more you respect yourself, [the more] others will follow suit. You also learned that your body is precious, and should not be abused by people, food, drugs etc. You learned that what you put into life is what you get out of it.

Nothing takes the place of hard work and commitment, but most importantly, you've learned to serve God with your whole mind, heart, and soul. God has blessed you to become a small business owner, performing poet, mother, wife, and friend to many. And that is why I am so proud of you."

A LOVE LETTER TO ME